THE
NEAR
WORLD

CARL DENNIS

WILLIAM MORROW AND COMPANY, INC.
NEW YORK

Thanks are due to the editors of the following magazines in which some of these poems first appeared:

American Poetry Review, "Charity," "The Chosen," and "The Dreamer";
Black Mountain II, "Matthew Remembers";
Brockport Forum, "Letter from John";
The Georgia Review, "Birthday," and "The Man on My Porch Makes Me an Offer";
The Kenyon Review, "Shakespeare in Delaware Park," "What Has Become of Them," and "Why Your Numbers Do Not Increase";
The Michigan Quarterly Review, "To Be Continued";
The New Republic, "The Embassy," "Flowers on Your Birthday," "The Veteran," "Later," "The Whole Truth," and "Hector's Return"; reprinted by permission of *The New Republic,* copyright © 1979, 1980, 1981, 1982, 1983, 1984 by The New Republic, Inc.;
The New Yorker, "The Midlands," "For Molly," and "More Music"; reprinted by permission; copyright © 1976, 1983, 1984 by Carl Dennis; originally in *The New Yorker;*
Pequod, "Captain Cook";
Poetry, "The Connoisseur," and "Steamboat Days";
Salmagundi, "At Home With Cézanne," "At the Corner," "Beauty Exposed," and "Puritans";
The Seattle Review, "The Mound Builders";
Skyline, "Strada Felice."

Library of Congress Cataloging in Publication Data

Dennis, Carl.
    The near world.

    I. Title.
PS3554.E535N4   1985   811'.54   84-27296
ISBN 0-688-04824-2
ISBN 0-688-04825-0 (pbk.)

Printed in the United States of America

First Edition

1 2 3 4 5 6 7 8 9 10

BOOK DESIGN BY SUSAN HOOD

For Martin Pops

THE NEAR WORLD

CONTENTS

IV

I

TO BE CONTINUED

Whoever we are when we finish the novel
Won't remember the details that are fresh now,
And if they can guess how much they've lost
They'll never write their review
And the characters will drift off unjudged.

Best to judge them now while beads of sweat
Are strung on Helen's forehead, after her ride
Around the lake. At thirty-four she's returned
To her father's farm—her brother's now—
A widow, determined to live in the past
No longer than she must, with no self-pity,
No remorse. It would be an act of ingratitude
To be sad by the lake of her childhood
Here in Chapter One, boating with nieces and nephews,
Docking on the island for a moonlight swim.

If we can trust her as we know we should,
She'll do us proud in every chapter to come.
We won't be outdone if our passion is compared
To the passion of the farmer across the road
Who's seen her only once, and from far off,
And has lost his heart already, and made a vow.

Hard to tell if he deserves her.
All we've been given so far
Is a single, unpromising paragraph.
At forty-five he's a drinker with a run-down farm.
Has love changed him enough?
Is the fever he runs in Chapter Two a dividing line?
Many chapters remain. Any one of them
Could drag him out of bed, back to the old plot,

Though he clings to the bannister.

We want to withhold our opinion till more facts are in,
But here he comes, stepping across the lawn
With scruffy flowers destined to impress her,
Given her large heart,
Which fills any blank with what it brings.

Nothing can stop the action. It's spring,
And the lilac is lavishing all it has
In smell and color on the empty air.

Only a minute to sit in judgment
On the pages read through so far
So the future that breaks in
Can prove us right or wrong,
Not merely older.

THE CONCERT

Heartening at the concert this evening
To hear the music rising up, unearthly, bodiless,
From glue and wood, catgut and horsehair,
From the voice box of the thick-necked, stumpy diva.
And back in my room it's inspiring
To hear the amateurs in the room above
Chugging away off-key through "Death and the Maiden,"
Four loudmouths during the day
Grown patient and serious
As they always do on Wednesday evenings.
And if, between movements, the cello player complains
That the other three are drowning his part out
When it's supposed to be loudest,
It's simply a sign of his struggle for the light
Which even the trees compete for.
And as the trees don't look at the bigger trees
Spreading across the valley and make comparisons,
These players don't compare themselves
With the great quartets they're able to admire.
They know what they are.
There will be no concert, not even for friends.
They imagine no ghostly ears as an audience
Listening from another planet past the wobbling pitch
To the pure intention, ghosts that may play
For other planets farther off, harder to please.
And God knows they're not playing for me,
The man who bangs on his ceiling with a broom handle
When they plod on past eleven,
Though sometimes I'm happy they don't stop,
Deaf to the world of noise I come from.
They're like the painter who turns her back on the traffic
And the skyscrapers looming behind her
To paint the harbor lights at dusk

And the graceful harbor birds.
The tall slabs of the city appear in the painting
Only in their shadows, long at this late hour,
Thrown on the water, as the birds,
Soaring and swooping, appear and disappear.

AT THE CORNER

This slender woman in the rain, rounding the corner,
Looks too determined for a trip to the store.
Maybe she turned on her porch a few moments before
And called back a few reminders to the baby-sitter—
If anyone calls she's shopping up the block—
Then hurried the other way. Now she's half done
With her journey crosstown to the tenements.
I can see her later as she climbs the four flights
And lets herself in with her key.
In the tiny room, dim beneath a bare bulb,
Her friend lies huddled in bed, coughing, his face to the
    wall.
Briskly she sets the table and boils water for soup or tea.

For an hour they discuss the real questions.
Is spirit unfolding itself slowly in history,
As Hegel argues, or holding back,
Camping out all year in open fields?
And why is spirit missing in the new novel
The woman recounts to her friend this week?
It makes her sad to meet characters who are not free,
Forced to embarrass themselves with a few narrow ideas
Recited on command, never to be revised.

The man sipping tea at the table agrees.
He sketches the plot of the fable he's been working on,
The Mermaid and the Carpenter, how the two meet on the
    dock,
Exchange a few words on the weather,
And suddenly love. Imagine the obstacles.

The woman tries to picture their house by the sea
As she walks home later,

Certain their blueprints can be reconciled.
And now the house floats into focus, its stilts and piers,
And the way there seems nearly as clear
As the way this tree on the corner, shining in the rain,
Calls up for me a long walk in the rain
With someone I believe was you.

HECTOR'S RETURN

By now he's died so often
And been dragged in the dirt so many times
It's easy. He'd have it no other way
And chooses with open eyes
To be deluded by his will to live
And press the attack on the ships,
To forget what he knew at the opening,
That Troy must burn, abandoned by its gods,
His wife and son doomed to be slaves,
His name lost among strangers.

It hurts me to see his mistaken hope,
Though I'm glad that the man I left last year
As ashes cooling on a funeral pyre
Has risen long enough
To fight Achilles once again and fall.
A poem that shows the generations of men
As frail as the generations of leaves,
That makes my solid city flutter in the wind
Like Troy and thin to shadows, as unreal
As my grandmother's village in Lithuania,
Burned down in the War,
Or as the farm she lived on here,
Paved over for a mall years back,
Is the same poem that's watered roses
In Priam's garden so they bloom still.
I turn the page and the trampled leaves
Float up again to the branches
And turn green. And it seems for a moment
That time is too weak a god to worship,
Another illusion I can put my hand through,

Not the last word, as I supposed.

We assumed Grandmother's muttering at the end
About waves and crossings
To be her dream of some longed-for,
Fabled afterworld,
Not guessing she was a girl again
Crossing the sea to us,
Eager to rejoin the long line
On Ellis Island.

CAPTAIN COOK

So often had he sailed the world in dream
That even the first voyage was more like homage
To the gods of repetition than like discovery.

The day the landbirds perched in the spars
After months of empty seas could have been many days.
Again through mist the steep headland
Or the same flat beach at dawn when the sky cleared
Or darkened. Always the excited crowds on shore,
The flotilla of canoes, the eager swimmers,
Young men and girls laughing among the ropes.

Today he may call their home New Zealand,
Tomorrow the Society Islands or Friendly Islands.
And this is Mercury Bay, Hawke Bay, or Bream Bay.
Time again for patching the wound in the main keel,
For refilling the water casks and exchanging cloth and nails
For pigs and fruit, rock oysters and yams.

Always the same trouble with island thieves,
The spyglass missing again, the quadrant, the anchor buoys,
More shovels, pulleys, bolts, and screws,
Till the worst offenders are driven off with small shot
Or flogged, and the sailors are flogged again
For not watching their muskets carefully.

Today as before the Captain rows after two deserters
And climbs the hill again to their leafy hideaway
And drags them from the arms of the weeping island girls
Back to the ship, and again the sailors wail

Like Odysseus's sailors dragged back from the lotus fields.

This captain is no Odysseus, no raider of cities.
He takes no booty as he claims an island
For the King, trying simply to fill
The white spots of his map with dots and lines,
Unseduced by a hunger for experience,
By the gospel of growing whole,
Patient like a man who's been everywhere
When the chief rows out to deliver his long
Incomprehensible speech of welcome,
Willing to hear him to the end and make in return
His own incomprehensible speech
And then rub noses, as is the custom there.

Not a part of all he meets, though no one is readier
To taste the boiled South Sea dog and the worm stew,
No one more impressed by the night-long paddle dance.
It doesn't matter to him how much or little his heart
Is written on by adventure as he writes in his log
His reckoning of the latitude, practicing the same skill
He practiced before in the same Pacific
Under the numbered phases of the moon
And the wheel of stars.

STRADA FELICE

for Burton Weber

April in Rome and Gogol rises from his desk
And looks down awhile from his balcony. The lamps are
 lit.
A cart rattles by on the cobblestones. Forty years old
And now, on this far street, the endless parade of towns
Of shapeless Mother Russia assembles in his head;
The lists of details stuffed in his trunk seem usable.
Now two servant girls outside Kostroma, their skirts tucked
 up,
Can wade in the pond with their nets, arguing,
And the farmhand can sleep off his vodka in the shade of
 the fence
As the hero's carriage totters up. It's go-getter Chichikov,
Jumping out in the dust with his calling card.
Any dead serfs for sale, he wonders, counting the huts.
Any names for his paper estate? A few dozen more
Should suffice to impress the mother of the rich girl.
Here's a ruble for the ghost of Peter the tinner,
For Stephen mender of sleds. Now back to the inn,
Past the clerks returning from their walks,
Past the women of the town in red skirts and furs, loi-
 tering,
None of whom are noticed by Chichikov, none described
In the letter not sent to a friend.

How strange his hurry seems to Gogol in Rome
Who holds these figures in his mind's light
So purely, as if sharpened by the miles.
Could they shine like this in Russia?
Wouldn't he lose them in the trees or the snow
If he started home, unless he brought Rome with him

And lugged its side streets and seven hills
Up the stairs on Great Meschanskaya Street
To the room beneath the rafters?
Then the books on Russia, piled on the floor,
Foreign so far, might sound, as he read them, like his own,
The lists of madmen and saints merely the names
Of his own moods writ large,
And he'd wonder why he waited so long
Before he ordered the Tsar to free the serfs,
Why he allows the pogroms to go on.

II

DAYS

The day comes like no other, the sun barely up
And the frost clarified into dew.
In the garage, the mower I assumed stolen
Has been returned with a note in a strange hand
Thanking me for the loan. Walking out to the front,
I see my lawn's been cut. It looks like a morning
To found the religion I've been hoping to found,
Based not on hope or fear but gratitude,
That will put Buffalo on the map
With Benares and Jerusalem.

Those who believe that only this morning is real
Will be my priests and dervishes,
My morning singers, as they go through each song once,
Coming together by accident for an hour
Under the awning of the corner fruit stand,
Jamming in the rain, then drift away
To other combinations.
The trouble in our church will arrive tomorrow
When they ask me to forget what I feel now
And live only in that fresher light.
Whatever I remember, they'll say,
Is the day's husk, not its flower.

Doubtless a fresh dream may come tonight,
One like no other,
A dream like Jacob's ladder, all promises.
Will Jacob abandon it for another dream
And forget the smell of the flowery field
Where he lay asleep, counting the angels
Climbing up and down, skirted in light?
Sitting in the garden of Joseph's house,
He'll smell it still,
The odor mingling with the fresh Egyptian flowers.

SHAKERS

Hard to believe no joy lived in the heart
Of the carpenter who made this Shaker desk and chair;
But the joy, our guidebook says, of a child
From whom all choice and trial is kept away,
Who passes the day in assigned chores and prayers.

And their quaking dances after the day's work
In shop and field, the leaping and the shouting,
Are said to have been graceless, the twisting of pinched flesh,
Bruised nature, though no one denies their plain,
Unaccompanied hymns are beautiful.

Not hymns of asking, only giving thanks.
Nothing to ask for if the Second Coming
Has already come, as they believed,
The thousand years of peace already begun.

What was hard before the light broke
On the bare walls was easy afterward,
The barren house suddenly home,
The best place for their thanks to echo in.

Only the shouters of commands or battle cries
Can't hear the news, and the silent ones
Who are still waiting, wondering what they're doing wrong.

THE MIDLANDS

In summer in our town,
When the ghost of Hamlet's father, stifled,
Wrenches from his grave, lunges up the road
Toward the hillside cabin of his son, the star-gazer,
Perched higher than the goats graze,
He tires halfway and sits down, panting, on a stone.
In the town below the streetlamps glitter.
The street noise thins to nothing as it climbs.
Listen as he might, he hears no cries of revenge
Among all the scraping of crickets and leaves.
After an hour what can he do but head home?
Meanwhile his son, undistracted, his eyes on the stars,
Hauls his blanket to the roof for a clearer picture,
Jots down his sightings, dozes off at dawn.

In winter in our town,
When white-haired wise men arrive
With handmade presents for the child,
They get lost in a bad district and are robbed.
It's snowing hard when they try to rise.
They stagger to the lighted door of the bar.
The barkeeper washes their wounds.
In the morning, waking in a beer haze,
They're too ashamed to go on.
So the child, never named, grows up ignorant
And copies the habits of his friends,
Tries to be last inside when his mother calls,
Jockeys for first place in line on the Sabbath
At the double doors of the Tivoli,
Whose double feature never seems to change.

MORE MUSIC

This one thinks he's lucky when his car
Flips over in the gully and he climbs out
With no bones broken, dusts himself off,
And walks away, eager to forget the episode.

And this one when her fever breaks
And she opens her eyes to breeze-blown,
Sky-blue curtains in a sunlit house
With much of her life still before her
And nothing she's done too far behind her
To be called back, or remedied, or atoned.

Now she'll be glad to offer her favorite evening hours
To Uncle Victor and listen as he tells again
How the road washed out in the rain
And he never made it to Green Haven in time
To hear the Silver Stars and the Five Aces.
And she'll be glad to agree that the good bands
Lift the tunes he likes best above them to another life,
And agree it isn't practice alone
That makes them sound that way
But luck, or something better yet.

And if Victor thinks he's a lucky man for the talk
And for his room in his nephew's house
Up beneath the rafters, and the sweet sound of the rain
Tapping on the tar paper or ringing in the coffee can,
Should we try to deny it? Should we make a list
Of all we think he's deserved and missed
As if we knew someone to present it to
Or what to say when told we're dreaming
Of an end unpromised and impossible,
Unmindful of the middle, where we all live now?

CHARITY

Time to believe that the thin disguise
On the face of the blessing in disguise
Will never be pulled off,

That the truth that's still in hiding
Will stay there, far in the dark.
All that can be revealed is revealed.

All that can be learned from the burning house
Was learned the first time, when the smoke
Blackened the walls in every room.

So much for more experience. What can grow
Has grown; what's small now stays small.
No portion waits for those who deserve more.

The flowers in the yard of the blind and deaf girl
Will never smell any sweeter to her
Than they smell now to any of her visitors.

The music she imagines will never compare to ours.
Her best day will brighten with no joy
That hasn't brightened our day more.

Time to admit that her steady cheer
Is the burden she assumes to keep us here
Touching her fingers for a while.

LETTER FROM JOHN

"We don't want troublemakers at Attica,"
The man said, so last month they moved me here
After seven years, north to Dannemora.
Otherwise I'd have written sooner.
I'm glad you liked my poem.
Your comments were helpful.
The stanza on death I can see now
Is overdone, said better earlier
In the figure of the flooded quarry.
I meant the woman in rags you ask about
As the moon, cloud-streaked that evening.
But the gray dust you take as metaphor
Is real. Dust from the concrete floor
Floats in the air all over Dannemora.
In the morning you see it clearest.
"Mottled green" is the color of the chipped paint
On the cell walls, which I contrast to the dark green
Of the one hill outside the window.

Hard to put into words what you feel
When the steel door slams behind you.
They drove me here through open country.
Huge skies stretched down to hills.
I saw the Hudson from the Newburgh bridge,
Clean and shimmering.

Handcuffs and leg-irons for two days,
Stripped and searched each night and morning.
They hate it if your back is straight.

The reference to the ocean near Montauk,
Though it seems to you dragged in from nowhere,
Suggests what the gray, forty-foot wall

Reminds me of. Not a perfect likeness, I admit,
A way not to bring the wall close but to push it back
For a spell of privacy, a little breathing room.

THE MAN ON MY PORCH MAKES
ME AN OFFER

"Above all houses in our town
I've always loved this blue one you own
With its round turret and big bay window.
Do you dream about it the way I do?
Wouldn't you be just as happy
On a street with more trees
In a larger house, whose columned porch
Impresses every passer-by?
Does it seem fair that you've won the right
To gaze from these windows your whole life
Merely because you saw them first,
And consign me to a life of envy?
I'll gladly assume more than your mortgage,
More than the new brickwork and roof repair.
Often I've noticed your wife and daughter
Waiting on the porch, peering down the street
For your car, a handsome, modest pair,
And I'm sure I can make them happy,
Happier than you can,
You who have other projects to work on.
I would live for you the one life
You'd have wanted to live, had you stayed,
And you can walk free, away from town,
Out beyond the suburbs, to that quiet place
Where the small voice of your true self
May be heard, if anywhere, and each day
You can wake up feeling your powers
Still increasing, which is happiness,
While I lose myself in the life you made
And did not want enough,
Happy when the space you left is filled."

NIAGARA FRONTIER

Not hard to find, ten minutes from Exit 53,
The only house on the block with a rooster weather vane,
And in the front yard lilacs and a Norway maple
With five trunks. That's our high window facing east.
On clear days the sun wakes us, burning through dreams,
And we dress quickly for work, as we do on gray days
When the dreams go with us.

Whether we liked this place at first
Or grew to like it, chose it from many
Or from one, the last one left,
We can't recall now. And what we were like then
Appears now as the blurred end of a dream
When the light pours in. Time to get up.
The painter's ladder is knocking against the house.
The painter will hum to himself all day,
Daydreaming of the hills above Palermo
Where he learned his trade, Tyrrhenian breezes.

Never once has this district turned its back on dreamers.
Two hundred years ago a few traders
Among the tribes, a trapper or two
Roasting a squirrel on a stick over coals,
Lying back to look at the stars,
Musing on Sara or Agatha in Vermont
And of the inn he hoped to manage one day
On the road to Boston.

Even the trees in August on Chestnut Ridge,
Where we glimpse the city floating beyond the farms,
Are not here only, but elsewhere too,
Their leaves already starting to turn,
Beech, black birch, sugar maple, and cherry

Ready to stand knee-deep in snow
As if winter were one of their favorite moods,
Time for meditation or for dream,
One act in the play they've staged so many times
They think they made it up.

Foolish of us to think that to grow in the sun
Was the only thing we wanted to do with ourselves,
That the passing hour by itself could feed us.
We hear it calling from far off
Like a child left alone too long,
And turn aside in our rambles, and circle back,
Willing to comfort it for a while.

THE HOUR

for Alan Feldman

Ten years from now the scene catching the eye
Of the boy as he leafs through Christmas cards
Will push him on his way to the snow country and a farm
Though then it will seem to him
The slow emerging of the life he saw once
Before birth in a dream
And chose before many others.

His father, looking up from the paper,
Can guess already that he won't succeed one day
In persuading his son to work in the store,
That whatever he's passed on besides life
And a little encouragement
Will remain invisible.

So why not forget that future and help his wife now
With the invitations for New Year's Day?
So many of the guests she hoped to greet
Have moved away with those she can't recall
That she has to move far down on her list.
For these she'll open the bottom drawer
Of the cabinet for the silver seldom used,
Reserved for a feast dreamed of as a child.

And this very minute they can watch their daughter
Step out to scatter crusts from the porch.
See how already she's forded the Mississippi
Between knowing that the birds are hungry
And wanting to feed them,
How she's crossed in a moment without a thought
The cold Atlantic between
Wanting to help and helping, .

As others up and down the street have crossed,
Leading the hour through the glittering snow
To the snowbound city.

No need to ask in what strand of narrative
This evening is an episode, and a minor one,
Now that you feel what you need to feel
To complete the moment as it eases into reach,
A moment for you so pure
It seems a moment for the world.

PURITANS

for Robert Daly

They wanted the big prize, bliss everlasting,
And knew they couldn't earn it, being human.
On the long chance they were chosen, or would be,
For reasons they knew they couldn't learn,
They prepared their hearts to receive
As saints would, and waited,
Wondering if their hour would come.
The Sunday morning when the gospel passage
Read like a letter from a friend,
Sweet and clear, may have been a true fall
Of heaven's grace, but maybe not.
Many despaired on their deathbeds, even ministers.
No words of hope in the sermon at the funeral
Though spoken by a friend; no angels
Carved on the headstone, only skulls.

Viewed from my desk, it seems their intensity
Was a crude recompense for their gloom.
Winters were more than snow and cold, were trials,
The loss of a child a sign to turn from the world,
And their grief witnessed and weighed and written down.

By the time my grandparents landed,
Pursuing happiness, they were long gone,
Their faith converted into history in the book
I've brought along today to the beach.
Hours of talk with friends in the sand,
And now the sun is sinking into the lake,
Shadowing forth no brighter sun rising ahead.
Will something be said tonight in the kitchen
To prove that the clouds and spray gone by

Are not so lost as they seem? Should I feel free
If I love the hour for itself?

Days I haven't wasted looking ahead
I've wasted looking back,
Reliving the day at the fair I was too scared
To ride the Comet, though friends rode,
Hair flying, seven times, and waved down.

Whatever the mood is called that pushes away
Remorse and longing, its coming leaves me grateful,
With the feeling my friends haven't been wrong
To trust me, that their eyes
Were as open as mine when I chose them.
A moment before, the stones strewing the ground
Looked unfamiliar, as if I missed the right road
Years back and can't return.
Grace comes for an hour and I'm sitting among ruins,
Noble ruins, and my own, with the outlines visible,
With enough time handy to begin again.

FLOWERS ON YOUR BIRTHDAY

I'd have been here sooner, believe me,
If the short cut across Jefferson Bridge
Hadn't been clogged by a funeral
And I hadn't counted the cars,
More than a hundred, most filled,
It seemed, with official followers,
Paying their respects to power.
Then, on the long way round, by the armory,
A burning house packed all the side streets
With fire-watchers. Half the city, it seemed,
Had nothing important enough to work on
That it couldn't be set aside for a fire.
And I watched it for a while, stared as a fireman
Scrambled to the third floor
To carry a girl down, and noticed that her dress
Was fringed like one of yours. And she looked like you,
A younger sister, smaller and more frail.
From there I drove straight here, bringing you
These flowers. See how fresh they are.
The black spots are merely soot from the fire,
Not symbols of anything, and will rinse away.
The afternoon, scattered with flowers,
Is all yours, wherever it leads.
And this evening we can go to an old movie,
A romance from the war, where the girl's wooed
By three brave officers, English, Russian, American.
It doesn't matter which she decides on.
They're all fighting on the same side. Her tears
Aren't an old woman's tears for a life that's spoiled,
Thrown away on a clod, but the tears of the young
Shed because she can only choose one
Of the dear, beleaguered lives held out before her.

FOR MOLLY

For him to remember what he was
Back in the days he knew the truth
You knew, loved what you loved,
Would be to bear on his back a grief
Too massive for the narrow door of his house
On the quiet side street, where his one wish
Is to sleep through the night unvisited.
So your face is airbrushed from the photograph,
Your name erased from the history book
Of his little country, the thoughts
That could testify on your side
Banished to a cold Siberian wilderness
To die unmourned for, with no witnesses.
You are the only archive now of a state too small
For any stranger to care how it once was ruled
In the old days, under the old king.

May a town that loves the truth
Be yours one day and invite your chronicling.
May you love the honest talk in the town square
And the gentle way the shoppers push through the aisles
With their shopping carts and exit to the lots.
The school bus stops at the crosswalk in the dark,
Its lights flashing, and the children climb aboard.
Your life may serve them as a guide, and later,
When they travel and can make comparisons,
They'll understand how rare their luck was.

But if no town receives you and you lose heart
And fall away from the woman you once were,
You won't pretend that she never lived, as he does.
You'll be sad to think how far you've come
From the customs of her country.
You'll be happy you can still remember her.

WHAT HAS BECOME OF THEM

Somewhere back in the lost place, you're still repeating
The same partial, uninspired replies to the girl
Who looks out the diner window in despair,
And your mother still wipes her eyes, still walks away
From the grave of her daughter,
And your dead father still searches for a house
Where bad thoughts can't force the door.

Once you thought these ventures finished,
Crumbled to powder, blown away. Now you know
They go on elsewhere as they were, unheard, invisible,
As the stream found in the woods, breaking on the rocks
In white water, continues to break after you've gone.

The sea wall washes away; the tree blows down
In the summer storm. But you still wake in the house
That burned to the ground years back
And turn to the arms of your young wife
In fresh joy, as if the fire were merely dreamed.

These moments are far now, farther each day,
But at night you make it to the town they live in
And watch them at their lighted windows
As they lose themselves in their parts
With the same emphatic gestures,
Not one word altered, not one left out.
They're too caught up to notice their audience,
And it doesn't matter if you stay to watch
Or drift to the spectral outskirts of tomorrow.

THE WHOLE TRUTH

Say they never loved me
And were merely too proud
After so many years
To admit their mistake.
Doesn't that mean my light by itself
Was enough to brighten my whole house
Here on the dark side of Buffalo?

And if it's only my ignorance
And my love of company
That make me believe the good moods
I find on waking have flown in
From far off like clouds from Canada,
Sailing over the lake to end a dry spell,
If they're my own creation after all,
Isn't that more proof
I'm a god's child, if not a god,
Resting on my porch in peace
On the seventh day
After the train squeaks by to Lackawanna?

And when the night comes over the roof
Whether I'm ready or not, and the stars rise
For their own reasons, and I'm not disconsolate,
Doesn't that mean my stars are rising too
With new reasons for my desires,
New words to describe the way my friends
Stand out from the crowd of shoppers on Arbor Day
With words of their own devising
Different from any I've made up so far?

THE CONNOISSEUR

If my father had praised me a little when I climbed the tree,
If when I swam the stream he hadn't looked away,
Maybe I wouldn't need your praise now
When I tell you what the still lives of Cézanne
Say about pears and pitchers, tables and tablecloths.
You could believe or disbelieve. I'd be happy enough
Making my point with a graceful gesture under the gray
    eyes
Of eternity, eyes like my own, but colder and more re-
    moved.

Maybe my father was trying to prepare me for the world
Where no one listens and hadn't learned what a hardy
    bloomer
The heart is if watered early. Not watered then,
It never gets enough, though replanted near a waterfall.

"Look at me," I called from the branches, calling up
In my father's mind, for all I know, his own cries as a boy.
Can I say he felt the likeness as a sad sign
He'd passed on his uncertainties?
He wasn't the kind who makes comparisons,
A brooder, with a cheerful face for his children,
Another for the dark of his own room.

More the kind who finds in a family outing at the park
With a dinner basket, a net, and a volleyball,
All he needs to complete his happiness;
The kind who says, "No matter what happens next
Nothing can touch this hour." It's all music for him—
The wind rustling the paper plates, my mother's voice
As she called us to the blanket, my cries from the tree

Mixing with the squeak of the crickets in the fall grass
While the airplane high in the clouds droned by.

That's how you might learn to hear my questions
With a little practice, as the soft hum of desire
When my eyes brighten on your return.
Soon I may hear it that way myself,
Not as a plea or as words at all,
But as the sound of brushstrokes at the bottom of the day
To complete the picture,
White moths fluttering beneath the stars.

THE EMBASSY

Just as I used to do when you slept beside me
I woke this morning with my own words in my ears,
Having dreamed again of speaking to the Senate,
Explaining just how easy it is
To help our sister republics to the south
Once we turn back the greed that engenders fear
And learn to enjoy the company of equals
Where no one has to swagger to feel proud.

I thought the dream had gone for good,
As you had gone, and now it's returned,
And I reach the harbors of Brazil and Ecuador,
Step out on the pier to music, wave to the crowd,
And deliver my speech on friendship from the north
And the brighter day.

And you are there in back, a little older,
Smiling, proud that I never became practical.
And then the speech is over
And the crowd goes back to work,
The farmers to the land, the fishermen
Back to the sea, where they'll search today
For a boat weeks overdue.
Did I happen to see it as I sailed in?
Do I mind going out to help them look?

A LETTER

I followed your advice, went over to Rushland
To see the sunrise, watched the sky shift from black
To gray and yellow above the roofs, to red
On the hills. Should I have noticed something else,
Taken the sky, say, as a metaphor, the stars my hopes
To be dimmed soon by a greater light lighting my way
Or as the likeness of the sun that's risen all along
Unseen inside me?

Most likely for you the sunrise
Is like nothing else, as any moment might be,
Each with its own colors, even a moment like this
At the breakfast table, your brief letter
Unfolded again by the blue plate,
The poinsettia perched behind it on the window sill.
Outside, the gray snow of the yard.
The leaves of the poinsettia seem to have turned to them-
    selves
To meditate, dreaming of a house
Where the day comes earlier,
Of windows facing south on trees in bloom.

Each tree from here to your home,
Bare as it is, you'd call a door
Open as wide to the moment as Buddha's bo tree
Or burning like the Burning Bush
But with no small voice required to make things clear.

I can describe the tree marking the spot
Where, if you were coming from the south,
You'd turn left by the river and angle up.
It might be dusk as you looked across the white fields,

Almost time, you'd think, for the night creatures you know well
To have their moment too, with their own night songs,
Dark, lilting strains I choose not to listen for,
Hoping to dream the night away.

AT HOME WITH CÉZANNE

When the phone rings down the hall, I let it ring.
I sit still in my study chair and go on reading
About Cézanne. Sarah will answer it.
Most likely it's for her, an old boyfriend
From high school, or her first husband,
Calling for more advice, attentive still.

Only this evening I learned that Zola and Cézanne
Grew up together in Aix-en-Provence,
Friends through their boyhood and beyond.
What a great log of a fact
To throw on an autumn fire and muse on
When my books grow dull, to think what encouragement
Passed between them on their day-long rambles.

Why should I worry if her heart is large enough
For them all? I should be proud
To hear her voice through the wall
Grow sad when the caller's voice grows sad
Or brighten as his brightens.

Though Cézanne in Paris found few friends
To be open with, he found a tribe of painters
To learn from, and that was enough,
The silent encouragement of high examples.

She'd tell me who the callers are
If I ever asked her.
Why should I sift the soil
If her roots sink deep enough

And the tree is flourishing?

It's too dark to see from my window
The dogwood we planted this year.
A breeze blows in the curtains.
It carries the smell of dry leaves
Falling on a street in Paris outside the Salon.
Zola and Cézanne are glad to walk out of there
And breathe the fresh air of fall.
They're not surprised that the judges
Threw out all the entries that were dazzling.

No doubt she's glad as she listens to the caller
To smell the leaves too
And remembers the girl on her father's farm
Jolting along on the pony I've never seen pictures of
Beside the haystacks and the clover fields.

WHY YOUR NUMBERS DO NOT INCREASE

At the hour you climb the stairs
Out of the world of your pains and pleasures
Up to the quiet chambers of the serious
And find the guidebook open on the table
To lesson one, "How to Love the Light,"
You hear the steps of someone climbing down,
Light steps, as if his heavy, golden book
Of duties, followed for years in detail,
Seems now to him a forgery.
And as you vow today to honor truth
He vows to live from now on for surfaces,
Pies and pearls, not for shadows,
And take in the party tonight in the Topaz Room
And try all the dances,
Those he knows and those he has to fake.

At the hour you love the woman
In the hand-framed photograph on the desk
With no hope of return, as you love the sunrise
Or the bright, oblivious women of Vermeer
Who live alone like worlds, complete, serene,
Someone brushes your door, rushing to the room
Where his love waits in the dark
Flushed with desire only for him.
Never again will he pause
At the window in the hall and watch the light
Burning across the street behind the curtains.
No one whose life is larger than his own
Has ever lived there.

At the hour you feel strong enough
To call the image in the mirror responsible

For any mess you make, for any mess of others,
The sound of shattering glass reaches your room
As someone casts off his craving to respect himself,
A task he never chose on his own
Or might never have chosen had he known more.

STEAMBOAT DAYS

Attention, easy to win now
If your story is amusing, was hard to win then
When you stood in front of the one class of the school
And asked your questions,
The students still worn out from the harvesting
Or still dreaming of the trip back from their uncle's
On the paddleboat.

And how hard to win attention
When you climbed the stairs of the boardinghouse
Clutching your sprig of yard flowers.
Waiting at your door till your long speech,
Forgotten in fear, returned,
You tried to calm yourself.
This moment will look small,
You said, on the world's calendar
Next to the laying of cable on the seabed
Or the driving of the Golden Spike.

When she called for you to come in, your speech,
Blurted out, seemed smaller than you remembered,
The room felt colder.
She looked up from her writing
With no smile. Your part in her plans
Was no bigger than the part of many others.
No need for explanations. Sorrow for you
Shown in her eyes as the silence stretched and grew thin.
Her few words were a sentence to return
To streets grown still and empty
And grow old in a ghost town.

But now the shops are open again; now you've been seen
Lounging with friends in the Chowder Restaurant,

Talking through the night.
Whoever promises to hold nothing back
Can join your table. A smile at yourself
As you push your hope into the dull light
Where it blinks with the others and grows commonplace
Leaves your soul clean and empty.

Remember how lonely you were in the old days
When you hoped no one would climb your steps
Till your message for the world had been clarified,
Your duties ranked and labeled;
When a favorite student had to prove himself
On a long trek, tramping through woods to your door?
If nobody knocked you walked alone by the lake
And watched the paddleboats.
There was always one, already loaded,
The steam hissing and heaving in the boiler.
The big wheel turned; the boat glided from the dock;
And a woman on deck waved to you in silence,
And in silence you waved back.

IV

LATER

Later you'll notice how slanted the floors are
And learn the meaning of the cracks above the lintels.
Now on the morning you move in
The dazzling, eastern light floods the big rooms.
The man who couldn't be happy here
Under these high ceilings won't find another place.

If you saw now what you'll see then
You wouldn't be moving in, though later
You won't regret your choice.
The bad news will arrive slowly and be different,
Not like a stranger's illness but a friend's.
You'll sit by his bed to cheer him up.

Then it's back to your study
To finish your novel about the lake.
Later you'll see how coarse it is,
Not the last draft, as you suppose now,
But the first. Be grateful for your ignorance,
For the gift of foolish confidence that allows you to begin.
Be glad the view of the road is blocked.
The trees are in the way, and the hill,
And the sharp jut of the lakeshore.

On the first day out with his boat,
Your hero, docked on the island,
Meets a stranger down on his luck
And invites him home.
Later you can make him remember
How small his house is,
How crammed with relatives,
All of them fretful as the years

Rub them the wrong way.
For now, as the breeze bellies the sails,
Let him imagine guest rooms waiting, and guest wings,
And months left at the doors like gifts,
May baskets, June boxes, July crowns,
August horns of plenty.

MATTHEW REMEMBERS

It was a custom where I lived for the women
In August to carry grain in red jars
Down to the salt pools of the bay
And light fires. The grain, sprinkled on the flames,
Gave off a sweet smell
And the wind blew it out to sea.

We had no legends of sea gods
Leaving their coral palaces
With sea nymphs dressed in bracelets of pearl
To rise for their gift of scented air.

We could smell it as we bobbed in the boats,
And then one of the old men would say
It's the time of the grain-burning again.
Could it be almost a year
Since Michael's last boy was born
And snatches of birthday songs blew by all night,
A year since Anna died in her sleep
And the slow echo of the bell reached us on the water?

SHAKESPEARE IN DELAWARE PARK

She makes me agree beforehand
Not to leave early if she does,
So I stay when she walks out at the break
After Act II, while Othello's faith
Is still spotless and Desdemona still smiles.

Someone behind us might guess she's glimpsed in the crowd
An old lover who spoiled a good beginning with jealousy.
Why sit here and let the play
Grate her with its coarse analogies?
But for her the hero is simply a man
In trouble who can't be helped,
A man she admires, sleepwalking toward a cliff edge
She'd never walk toward. She wants to call from her seat
To warn him. Let him choose a plot
Less slanted to catastrophe.
Why should she stay to be told
What she knows already, that she has no power?

The distance from her seat to the stage
Isn't far enough. Am I sitting farther away
When I stay to watch him stumble?
Am I so in love with the beauty of the probable
That I want a simple soldier to be fooled
By the simplest strategy, a handkerchief and a lie,
And receive full strength the fate of fools?

I hope I'm waiting for his high, improbable words
As he staggers under a blow
That should leave him speechless,
Proud words with masterful arguments,
With phrases crowded with comparisons,
Beyond all natural, mute anguish and stammering,
The squeak and rattle of the plain style.

SHADOWS

In Memory of John Gardner

Now when I open your last novel
I can almost look past the hero's likeness to you
And watch, undistracted, as he drives up the hills from
    school
In his rusty pickup, ranting at destiny; almost free myself
To enter the dream you thought all art must try for
And smell the grass he smells at the hill's crest
And find that the smoke blowing from town makes my
    eyes water.

Now in the hill house he can't afford, unable to explain
His debts or divorce, or the move from his old house and
    town,
Unable to write, he sits at his desk
Rereading Nietzsche's sparkling arguments
Against reason, how feeble its power is
To support the fictions that support the world.

Till now, though he's liked how Nietzsche resists belief
And embraces the cold gospel of honesty,
He's tried to resist his dark moods,
Hoping one day to bridge the dubious visible world,
That might mean nothing, with the world desired,
Trying to arrive in Vermont and California, New York
And Illinois, planting peach trees and apple trees,
Joining the local orchestra in the fire hall.

Now he lives as far from the world as he can
In his empty hill house. But look at how big it is,
However remote, too big for one man.
Look how he's challenged by the rotten clapboard
And the walls fallen from square to become a carpenter

And convert the shed in back to a dining room.
If only, after a day spent plastering, he didn't wake to
  whispers
As a crone and codger, hermit inhabitants buried years back,
Grope in the dark by his bed, wringing their hands.
If only a murdered student didn't phone for a grade.

The dark drives him down the hill again,
Praying that the friend he's looking for
Hasn't been changed to someone else,
That her town will still be there and real, not a ghost town,
Though its lights clustered below look small:
Candles afloat in a black sea;
Campfires circled by wolves or trolls.

He finds the windows of her house all lit,
The whole cast of characters gathered for the finale
With an orchestration of key words and images
It seems every story should try to end with.
But how can his friend's dead husband be waiting on the
  porch?
How can the rooms be full of unseen voices,
Bird-like and lynx-like as well as human,
While the windows shake in a shower of bones,
Unless he's gone at least half mad?

Had I called your house, as I'd planned, for explanations,
I'd have pulled you from your new novel,
The one where you let your fears finally run wild.
How is it coming, your plot roomy enough at last
For the wildest characters and barely half done?
Is the killer still closing in on the heroine?
Do we learn soon why he's after her?

Soon or not soon; that means nothing now.
Nobody's pulled away from the desk in the dark house

When the phone rings. The old detective, a cynic and a
    drunk,
Will try forever, despite his ideas, to protect his client
And never learn for sure what he's up against,
Forever afraid he can't help, the case too much for him.

THE DREAMER

If the dream I dreamed was mine,
Why have its images remained so veiled,
As if a face had turned away?

This must be a dream that was heading elsewhere.
In the dark it missed the appointed house,
Whose owner would have no problem with its episodes—
The bear asleep on the loading dock of the mill
And the girls in yellow circling the courthouse
With cherry branches, singing.

These are not images from my childhood,
Not tokens of my future, but the future of all who live here.
Someone who feels that the problems of his people
Are greater than his own
Is waking now unsuccored by a dream.
From his window he looks down on the courthouse square
And notices what he's noticed before,
A few dogs, a few stray cars,
A scatter of early shoppers,
And guesses that a light has been withheld.

Meanwhile, the bear and the girls,
That should have been his, are not explained.
Those who need the message are growing old.
They are turning away, as guests at the ocean hotel
Turn from the beautiful unnamed fish
Stranded in the tidal pool
Back to the supper on the lawn,
The supper stories, the badminton and croquet,
All dreams as well, and smaller and more frail,
But pushing forward to be chosen before nightfall
With no need to explain themselves.

BEAUTY EXPOSED

At the bookstore you wait for the new clerk,
The beautiful one, who sold the books you ordered
To someone else, though the plain one
Brings you what you need unasked.

Not wanting to feel guilt, the Greeks
Made beauty the gift of a goddess,
Called their love for fine features piety.
And Plato, straining to prove man rational,
Argued that to love the beautiful
As all men do is to love the good,
The two one in the spectral world
Of metaphor, where the question's begged.
Here where we live, in the cave,
Nobody's fooled.

And nobody's foolish enough to believe
It lives only in the beholder, as personal
As your taste for the ginger cookies
Your mother made, which no one else liked.
Too much agreement for that and for too long.
The statues in the museum aren't exchanged
Each year for new ones. They stay,
And we find new reasons, new ways to explain
Why they wake the flesh in the old way.

All our heads turned in unison
When the girl in the blue dress entered
And walked along the library aisles
To the section on law and kneeled
Or stood on her toes, hair flung back.
Before she uttered a word we could look behind,
Before an action we could dream up motives for,

We had to sit confounded by the surface glare
Of the visible, frightened to be so far
From the dark world we understand.

BIRTHDAY

In the life to come, in the field sloping down
Back of the summer house I still haven't seen,
Where I love to walk with the friends
Whose faces I can't yet recognize,
Let night fall soon, let fog blow in
And blot the ghostly porch light that a moment ago
Shone like the stern lamp of a ship.
Let me turn back to these porch steps
Chosen long ago to rest on
Till I caught my breath.

Then as I enter the house, let me believe
My trip to the dream place only my way
Of stepping back to admire this handiwork.
Let me feel that my hands,
Closing on the knob as they always have,
Have always closed on the world
And should waste no time now
Breaking the habit, learning to let go.

THE VETERAN

Once it was hard to believe
That the birds I watched for hours,
Darting and perching, had no opinion
About me, and would have none.
Now I'm tranquil even if my city,
Known far longer, doesn't look my way.

If my strengths and weaknesses aren't needed here,
I can imagine a city where they are.
Here the people may contend I haven't done enough
To free the light from the dark of history.
But there they'll say I'm helping
Even as I sleep, like the sleeping,
Oblivious trees where the birds are singing.

If the mercy of the angels I dreamed of yesterday
Long ago ran out, if I used it up,
Today I dream of angels with an endless supply.
It's their vocation to come up with it;
It's a challenge they run to meet;
It's how they enjoy themselves.

I was knocking at my own door yesterday.
I was looking in the window, wondering
Who could live in this small room,
So plain and empty. Today I stand inside
And look out, mindful of the trees,
The birds, the planet.

If I can't tell what will happen
It's because I'm free. The birds
Will always be birds. They can't stop.
I could forget myself in a minute
Even now if I stopped dreaming.

THE MOUND BUILDERS

for Philip Schultz

Campers are digging again on Tamarack Hill.
They must have found so little company during the week
Among the living that they'll settle on the weekend
For refuse of the dead—pot shards,
Buckles of bone, beads, arrowheads.
Maybe they hope an image of a new life
Will turn up in the mud, a little jug
Intact, with a shaman's scroll inside,
A diagram for aligning their house
With the axis of the stars,
A few hints on the language of animals.
Every crumb of truth is useful, they might say,
Since the whole loaf was broken up.

And if, after months of knee-gouging slow work,
They meet with no luck, they're not annoyed.
They don't walk off the job.
If they dig now, someone after an age
May dig them up in return,
Someone more eager than they are,
More imaginative, who won't need much encouragement.
They won't have to finish the town hall for him.
All he'll ask is a stone or two
And his own need will do the rest,
Multiplying the stones like the loaves in the miracle.

And if his needs are met already
And he lives in a starry city
At home with the light of constellations
And with clouds that block the light,
Let him find in the dirt a window shaped like a star
Or a star in the buried bricks of the patio
And imagine we dreamed of a city like his

Where men from the Street of the Archer
Wave to women from the Street of Scales
As they pass in the market, searching for bargains,
Or run through the rain to the awning of the small arcade
To wait at their leisure for the sky to clear.

THE CHOSEN

She lives by Cherry Hill where the dirt road
Drops down to the west across the valley.
Her husband has the egg route there.
After she walks the children to the bus
She weeds the garden, hangs out the laundry.
In the evening she reads by the warm stove
Or walks into town. She belongs to the choir.

If I see her night light from the road,
A star in the window,
It seems she's hung it there for a friend.
Whoever needs her when the moon is gone
Can find the hill path.
Before he reaches the porch
She wakes to his footsteps on the gravel,
Slides out from beside her husband,
Draws on her robe and goes down.

If he's come to tell her how his work
Has faltered this year,
She'll point to a few promising lines
And urge him to interpret his gloom
As the key to his true calling,
His hunger for perfection.
If he tells her how he hates his life here,
Hates every nail and board in town,
She'll tell him not to fight his heart anymore
But to follow it and feel what the Jews felt
Under Pharoah by the Nile,
A true calling not to settle down,

Not to feel at home.

These are the words he's come to hear.
He can leave the porch now,
Free as he goes to wonder
How she's managed already to build her house
In Canaan and dig her well
In its promised soil.

TIME HEALS ALL WOUNDS

The first wound, the cut at the cord stem,
No longer tender, the scab fallen off,
The baby no longer sleeping with its knees
Tucked up, dreaming of the dark,
But reaching for the window on belly,
Elbows, and hands, on feeble frog legs;

The cut closed in the boy's head
Received as he ran back for the catch,
Not hearing as the fielder called for it
Or hearing but not believing the ball
Destined for anyone but him;

Pain gone from the wrist
Sprained when the enemy stormed the camp
And tore the flag from the guard's hands
While the guard played dead,
Thinking how unfair it was
For the good side to be so outnumbered;

The tear in the hollow of the thigh
Where the angel touched it and the holy,
Aspiring sap of the wrestler
Leaked out, wetting the ground,
Feeding the seed of a flower whose smell
No one alive remembers, all healed now;

The wounds in the back
Where once the wings joined the body
Healed, and the legs grown used
To the whole weight.

About the Author

Carl Dennis was born in St. Louis in 1939. He now lives in Buffalo, where he teaches in the English Department of the State University of New York. Mr. Dennis is the author of three previous books of poetry: *A House of My Own* (George Braziller, 1974), *Climbing Down* (George Braziller, 1976), and *Signs and Wonders* (Princeton University Press, 1979).